Virtual Summit Profits
The Complete Playbook

LEONARD PAYNE

Copyright © 2019 Leonard Payne

All rights reserved.

ISBN: 9781703748741

DEDICATION

To my dear wife Lynne who supports me and to whom
I'm trying to keep in the style to which she
would like to become accustomed.

CONTENTS

INTRODUCTION	1
WHAT IS A VIRTUAL SUMMIT?	3
BENEFITS TO AN ENTREPRENEUR	5
YOUR LIST – THE MOST IMPORTANT FACTOR	7
BEST PRACTICE - SMALL BUSINESS SUMMIT	9
BEST PRACTICE – ONLINE BUSINESS	11
FINDING YOUR AUDIENCE	13
FINDING YOUR PRESENTERS	15
AUTOMATION	17
YOUR SUMMIT VENUE	19
OUTSOURCING DURING YOUR SUMMIT	21
MONETIZATION	24
REVERSE ENGINEERING THE PROCESS	26

ACKNOWLEDGMENTS

To all who have assisted, known and unknown I give thanks.
All the errors are mine alone.

INTRODUCTION

Welcome to **Virtual Summit Profits.** In this introduction, we are going to be doing an overview of the book, showing you how to build authority and profits from scratch and we'll be discussing the online business model, which revolves around creating a series of online speakers or otherwise called a virtual summit. Now, this has been done on those markets within the internet marketing or business opportunity niche, but the method is easily suited for any niche and in fact works even better outside of traditional make money online markets. Now, in chapter one we'll define what a virtual summit is and discuss how it differs from other online meetings. In chapter two we'll discuss how it can benefit you as an entrepreneur and why you need to consider doing one.

In chapter three, we'll discuss the single most important objective in planning a summit. In chapter four we'll then discuss how you do a summit for small and local brick and mortar businesses. In chapter five we'll take an in depth look at doing a summit for online businesses. In chapter six we'll discuss the different aspects of finding your audience. And chapter seven we'll discuss finding presenters for your summit. In chapter eight, we'll discuss how to automate different parts of managing your summit. In chapter nine we'll talk about where to hold your virtual summit or your venue. In chapter 10 we'll discuss different parts of maintaining your summit so that you can outsource them.

In chapter 11 we'll get into the monetization of your virtual summit, and in chapter 12 we'll wrap up the course by talking about some specific examples of virtual summits. So with that, thanks, and I will see you inside.

WHAT IS A VIRTUAL SUMMIT?

In this chapter we're going to define what a virtual summit is. A virtual summit is a seminar with multiple speakers speaking on a specific topic and it's going to be delivered to a target audience. Now any time that you do a virtual summit, there are going to be typically three sets of people involved. The first is going to be the audience and obviously they're coming either to get more information about this specific topic or they're looking to solve a specific problem and they're coming to hear multiple speakers on this topic.

Then you have the presenters, so you're going to be able to go out and get people who can either talk about different aspects of your topic or different ways of looking at the topic. You want to be able to think about this in a way that you are going to get a broad perspective of people who can cover the issue and really give the people who are going to be coming to your summit great value. And then you also have the organisers and the moderators. And for the most part this is going to be you, the person who is going to be operating the summit and other people who are going to be doing it with you. If you do a virtual summit with someone else and you do a summit and you are outsourcing, you are going to have people who are going to run the summit.

You're going to have people to make sure that the speakers have what they need to make sure the attendees have what they need. You are going to be making sure that these groups all come together in order to deliver a quality experience. Now in a virtual summit, this entire event is typically going to be free. And this is important to discuss. Some entrepreneurs, when they do a virtual summit, they will charge the people to come. In other words, they will set a price upfront for people to come and then they'll typically distribute some of those funds to the speakers. But, but for the most part, you're probably going to do a virtual summit and it's probably going to be free. Now we're going to talk about how you're going to monetize that summit later on in this course, but you can actually do a virtual summit if you can bring people to a location and online location that you are going to be able to build great authority as well as profits.

BENEFITS TO AN ENTREPRENEUR

Now in this chapter we're going to discuss how a virtual summit could benefit you as an entrepreneur in so many ways Now if you have an email list or contact database but it's not growing as fast as you want or it's not big as you would like it to be, a virtual summit is a great way of being able to do that because you are going to be leveraging the traffic that comes along with a desire to hear the speakers you're putting together as well as the tribe of the actual speaker or their following and so you're going to get the benefit of having some of those people come to this summit and then join your email marketing list.

You can benefit from a virtual summit even if you have never been asked to speak or present an event. What you are doing is you are bringing together the kind of person that gets asked to speak and then you are going to be in the same company. You're going to get some of the benefits of associating with them. Now, an online survey can benefit you if you aren't making enough sales of your products. And some of this goes to the fact that you are going to have more people to your list, but you're also going to be bringing these people to your site where as they start clicking around and looking, they're going to have exposure to your products and your service.

Now, a virtual summit can benefit you as an entrepreneur even if you don't get asked by vendors to promote their product. So what you're going to be doing is you're going to be giving exposure to other vendors who actually have products and what's going to happen is they're going to be more than willing and they're going to be more open to you promoting their products.

Sometimes you can approach a vendor and because they don't know you, you could be on delayed commissions or in some cases that vendor might not approve you at all, but once you are actually known by the vendor, you stand a much better chance of being able to promote their product whenever you want to.

Now a virtual summit can benefit you as an entrepreneur if you are already unknown in your niche or industry. You are going to be again associated with people who are known and will be known for their knowledge of the topic. You're going to be associating with them and you're actually going to be bringing them together, which is a fantastic way of building authority. Now, a virtual summit can benefit you as an entrepreneur if you don't like the idea of podcasting or blogging or writing and podcasting, blogging and writing are great ways of being able to create content that people want. However, they do require an ongoing commitment and in some cases as an entrepreneur you may not want something that feels like a job. Having a virtual summit is actually an event. It's an event that people need to come to and even sometimes a podcast or blogger writer, they'll do their own summit.

A summit again is an event and because you don't need long term permission, you might get better responses from the people who are going to be presenting. And a virtual summit can benefit you as an entrepreneur if you aren't necessarily that good at closing sales, so you're not going to have to make the hard sale by bringing someone to your virtual summit. They're going to have exposure to your ideas are going to have exposure to you so that you can be likeable. They're going to have exposure to your products and services when they come to your site. You don't have to necessarily be as good if you can make sure that through your summit you're really attracting a great audience as well as a great speaker set. A virtual summit can benefit you as an entrepreneur. If you already have knowledge or a passion that you want to share, you are literally going to be able to get in front of the people who matter the most to you in terms of your niche, in terms of your product and your service. So if you already have knowledge and you're just looking to expose that, expose that knowledge to the light of day and expose that knowledge to other people in order to interact with them. A virtual summit is a great way of bringing them together.

YOUR LIST – THE MOST IMPORTANT FACTOR

In this chapter, we're going to be talking about the most important factor to doing a virtual summit and that's going to be building and maintaining your email marketing list. It really is the single most important factor in organising any summit. You want to make sure that everyone who's coming to that summit becomes part of your email marketing list. You want to do whatever you'll have to arrange in terms of the technology to make sure that becoming part of your list is part of the signup process. Now this is going to mean that your autoresponder will need to integrate with your platform, so whether or not you're using a platform like webinar fusion pro or go to webinar, you will want to make sure that your autoresponder is very closely tied to the signup process. Now, one of the things you want to think about is whether or not you want to have single or double opt in leads.

Now you'll want to consider having double opt in leads if possible. First, even though there's going to be a drop off in terms of the number of people that joined to be keeping on your database, the autoresponder companies, technology typically puts them in a higher classification. These emails are more likely to be delivered over time than single opt in emails. So what that means is that you'll want to make sure that any handouts you do, any extras or any additional material that people are going to be getting, that they're going to be subject to opt in. Or in other words, the only way they're going to get these supplementary materials is they do have to opt in to get it. Because you want to make sure, do everything that you can to make sure that you get a double opt in lead from this process.

Now, make sure to sell the opt in by giving the visitor a good reason to want to give up their email. So let's say that you actually have gotten them on to the summit and the first page they see, you want to give them some reason to want to opt in. You want to give them some reason to make sure that they give you their best contact information. And typically, this can be your slides. It can be an additional bonus. It can be a get started or a quick start video. You want to do something that you can in order to inspire people to move forward. Now also, remember this, it's likely that your guests during their presentation will want to invite people to their opt in. So what does that mean? That means that you want to avoid selling your optin at the same time as your guest, or your presenter is selling their optin because you don't want your visitor to be confused. So you want to do yours perhaps at the very beginning, but certainly not the end of their talk or even at the conclusion. Make sure that you time your request, you want to make sure that it is as far away from your presenters pitch as you can possibly make it.

BEST PRACTICE - SMALL BUSINESS SUMMIT

In this chapter we are going to be discussing how you would go about putting together a summit for small businesses. Now in this particular case, when you are going to execute this strategy, you'll have presenters. So you're going to actually be able to go out and get people who are going to be speaking at the summit and you will obviously be the organiser, you and those who will be moderating the event. Now you are going to be talking to the heads of associations and organisations who are consistent with your niche. So in this particular case we've indicated that by saying in the chart that you'll be talking to the heads of trade associations. However, if you are in a particular niche, you're going to want to go to the top person of influence. You're going to be working with small local brick and mortar businesses and of course the trade association will be bringing you the audience and attendees. So they're actually going to go out to those who associated with their group and they are going to be inviting the attendees. Now, that's not to say that you will not be going out to get those attendees yourself and promoting your event, but the primary source for the audience, any attendees will be the trade association. As a matter of fact, once you've actually spoken with the trading association, you are going to be going out to get the presenters based on their particular needs. Now in order to execute this strategy, it's a good idea to listen to the audio book called networking with millionaires by Dr. Thomas Stanley. It'll actually outline the strategy and show you the benefits of it in detail.

Now you'll also benefit by having the Gayle's directory of local and regional associations. When we talked about going to get those trade associations or the people who run them, this is where you'll be able to find that information. Now if you are in a different market and you are not looking at small brick and mortar businesses or local businesses, then you're wanting to go to the trading association or the group that would have the audience that you want. And what you're going to do is a webinar series for this group association or a niche organization.

Now as an alternative, you can do an award series with speakers for particular group or a niche and you would then get professionals and authors who want to be in front of that niche. So in other words, you will match the presenters with the audience that you are going to be bringing together. Then once you have good presenters, you will get the group to promote the series. So in other words, what you're going to do when you go to get the presenters for the trade association, you're going to let them know who that's going to be and then you're going to ask them to promote to all of their members so that you will have a great attendance to your event and you will have a good opportunity to build your marketing list. Which brings us to the last point, the number one thing as we have said in other videos is that you want to make sure that you are capturing leads for this event because it is there that you'll actually make up for the time, money and effort that you're putting in on the front end of this event.

Now another thing that you can do is to offer sponsors the opportunity to be mentioned in exchange for a payment to you. That means then that you are going to give sponsors the opportunity to be mentioned, the opportunity to have their list built and you are going to give them the opportunity maybe even to do a short presentation in your summit and then they are going to actually compensate you in some way by either giving you some kind of payment or some kind of discount that will really matter to you and your organisation. Now that's the best practise if you are going to be working with small and local brick and mortar businesses. Now in the next video we're going to be talking about how you do this. If you are going to be working with online businesses in particular, delivering summits to them. So with that, thanks. And I will see you in that next chapter.

BEST PRACTICE – ONLINE BUSINESS

In this chapter we are going to be discussing the summit strategy if you're going to be executing it among online businesses. Now you'll see there that you still have presenters. Obviously you're going to have to go out and get presenters for your summit and you are still going to be the organiser, you and whatever moderators you choose and you are actually going to be going to try to do what you can to get the audience. Now of course, you'll be looking for your presenters to do some of the work for you by bringing the people that are already following them. Now let's talk about the best practise for this strategy.

Now in this case, the players or the presenters already have the list that you want to leverage. They already have a following. They already have the people in the niche that you want to reach with your product or service. Now you will need to have an influence list and that means then that you'll need to have people that you want to go after to be your presenters who are already connected with other people were going to be your customers. Typically you're going to want to have a list of about 100 and when you contact these people, this should not be the first time you've ever come across them. At minimum you should have purchased one of their products. Now as an alternative, just as we said in the other video regarding small brick and mortar businesses, one of the ways to do your summit is to do an award series with speakers for a particular group or niche or even topic. Now in terms of speakers, you want to get professionals and authors who want to be in front of your niche. Of course you want them to have a following because those are going to be the people that you are going to leverage.

Now, once you have good presenters, you are going to get the group of presenters to promote this series. And of course you are going to have to do a lot of promotion yourself. One of the keys to this strategy is for you to be able to bring as many people to the event as you possibly can, even if you have to go as far as to create paid advertisement. Now one way to get the players to be a part of your summit is to arrange for their affiliate link to be coded at 100% commissions for the product that is sold after the summit. And we're going to be talking about monetization. And this is going to be key when you want people to come, but maybe they're not necessarily feeling all that good about participating. You want to do everything you can to make it comfortable for them to participate.

FINDING YOUR AUDIENCE

In this chapter we're going to be talking about how you are going to find your audience. Now if you already have a mailing list, you will be the primary resource for the audience that will be coming to the summit. You are going to promote your summit to your email marketing list to your social media following and everyone who has contact with you. You are going to be promoting the event to them, and if you don't have an email marketing list, you'll be dependent on the speakers to bring their audience to the summit. Now even if you do have an email marketing list, you want to have the speakers to bring their audience because that is really the true leverage in doing a summit. Now you can also run Facebook ads to your landing page and go after a targeted audience for your summit.

You want to make sure that you have a match between the people who are going to be interested and the people that you're trying to attract to actually come to your free summit or your paid summit. You want to promote your summit in places where your audience hangs out online. Of course that means social media, but you also want to take a good look at forums and blog and when I mentioned blogs here, you do have the opportunity to guest post. You do have the opportunity to have a blogger mention you, and of course this is where having relationships prior to doing the summit is really going to help you in being able to build an audience for an actual event. Another thing that you'll want to consider is doing press releases and appearances on relevant podcasts and interviews shows or blogs and consider recruiting these people as your affiliates.

So in other words, one of the things that you can do, and we'll talk about this in another video, is that you can offer the people who were going to give you that exposure. You can offer them a higher commission if they choose to promote your product, that you can definitely give some kind of consideration to them. Maybe you'll have them plugged, but you definitely want to involve them by getting on and having them tell their people about this summit. Now if you are going to have an information product connected to the summit, you want to start approaching affiliates, that'll get a sale for referring their list to your summit. So you want to do this ahead of time. This is pretty important because this will actually not only bring traffic to the summit, but it'll also help you with sales after the actual summit and it'll help you to monetize the summit.

In this case, you will want to consider giving those affiliates 100% through the entire funnel of products and services. And this is the added incentive for them. Not only get people to the summit, but also to make sure that they do what they can to get people to stay till the end. So having affiliates work with you because they have an incentive to earn --- that will help people to get to the summit. It will actually help them to get onto your email marketing list and you will actually be paying for traffic. But you will not be paying for it upfront. You'll only be paying the traffic when someone actually makes a sale. You'll get the lead because the affiliates will send them to you and you'll be paying the affiliates on the back end, but you will still have the lead in order to use in your business.

FINDING YOUR PRESENTERS

Every summit is a two way street. A big audience will attract good presenters and good presenters will attract a big audience. So let's talk about now finding your presenters. Now to find them. You are obviously going to want someone who can deliver good content over and above everything else. This is going to be vital. You don't want this to be your first and last summit. You don't want people to come and feel as if they've been sold to and they'd been pitched to. You want to make sure that the people, even if they choose to make an offer or invite people to come back to their email marketing list, that they are delivering fantastic content and giving the people who've taken their time to come to the summit. Great value. Of course, the most important thing as we've said in the past is that you want people who are going to be fairly connected to an audience already.

If they put on social media that they're going to be presenting on a summit or that they're going to be doing a webinar, then you want them to be connected enough so that when they share that kind of thing on their social media or among their following that they'll actually have people to come. That'll be new to you and new to your business. Now, if possible, you want to think about those kinds of presenters that the potential audience, the people that you want to get onto your email marketing list, that they're going to recognise it. They're going to say, wow, that's a person I really want to hear. And inside of a specific market or specific niche, you can actually do that. So they don't have to be recognised names in pop culture or large society. They only have to be recognised names inside of the niche and that will attract people to the summit.

You want to have someone to see the name of this presenter. It's either the presenter and say, Oh boy, I have to take my time out and I have to be there. So at a glance, when you have the names of your summit, do they say to your audience, have to be there. I have to find time. I have to put things aside in order to be there. That is the true value of a summit to someone. If they don't know you, they'll come to your summit. For the other people, you can use PR sites like "help a reporter" and "find any celebrity". Again, those are great sites that you can use in order to get in contact with people that may be willing to be your presenter and we'll have that audience to come with them or will be able to attract an audience based on their name alone.

Now this is a case and we've said this in other videos, but it's really vital here. You will want to start building relationships long before summit and sometimes that's going to mean buying a product of someone that you know you're going to want to have of this summit or it's going to mean reaching out to them on social media and really getting to know them and following them or reading their work or sharing the stuff that they're already doing. It could mean actually just commenting on some of the things they do and interacting with them and expressing an interest, building relationships. Now when you do this, of course you want to be genuine. You want to be looking to someone because they really are interesting and you really do find their content or what they're sharing to be something that is of interest to you.

You don't have to do this in a way that's going to be disingenuous. You can be genuinely interested in what they're doing because those are going to be the people that you're going to be most excited about promoting. So think about this in terms of people that you really want to have at your summit. Yes, they'll be connected. Yes, they're going to attract an audience, but you want to be excited about them too. They should be the kind of people that you want to build a relationship with and that you enjoy talking to. Because if you enjoy talking to them, more than likely the people who are going to be in your audience, the people that you are already attracted who come to the summit that you invite, they're going to be interested in those people too.

AUTOMATION

Do go and checkout "Scheduleonce.com". This website will allow you to set up an appointment system and what it will do is it will manage every part of your appointment process. Now schedule once will integrate with whatever calendar system you use, so whether or not it's outlook or maybe it's Google or Apple, as soon as you make an appointment it will be placed on your online calendar. Somebody cancels it, it'll be taken off. This is really what makes the process really work because you can actually dictate where your schedule has availability and this is really what automates the process. You don't really have to send emails back and forth in order to find the right time.

You just send out a schedule link through schedule once. And the other integration we talked about is Zapier and Zapier actually allows you to connect to online, let's say online applications that otherwise would not integrate. So for example, if you wanted to connect, "GoToWebinar" to "GetResponse".

What you can do is you can have it so that when somebody signs up with GetResponse, they can be placed on your go to webinar. You can actually do it the other way around. And there are lots of other integrations that are like this between various online applications that you can actually tie together.

Now, Zapier is a paid application and you will be paying for every one that you actually do, but it's a nominal fee for the integration that you're going get if you're going to be building your list.

You will also need sime online pages or webhosting you can use. You should pick the one that's going to fit into your business model or fit into your budget and then use it. You're going to use these pages because you're going to need registration pages, you're going to need opt in pages. You're going to need to be able to put them together fast and to make them professional.

YOUR SUMMIT VENUE

In this chapter we are going to be talking about your summit venue. Now there are several ways to do this online summit. First, you can actually hold the summit on "GoToWebinar". Go to webinar is a service that costs $99 a month for 100 seats. Of course, if you need more than that, that you can pay more. Now the upside to go to webinar is that it's well recognised by people around the industry. The downside is it is fairly pricey unless you have a legacy account, so you want to start thinking about whether or not "GoTowebinar's" going to be in your budget, make sure that you check the pricing and then also check for any discounts that might be available.

The second technology to consider is "Zoom" Meetings. You can get upto 100 attendees in a 40 minute meeting for Free or you can get a higher profile for around $32 per month. Check all their offerings. The technology is fairly sound

The third area to consider is Google Hangouts Technology. There are many front-ends to this which help you use it. Upsides is that it is totally free. Downsides is that its pretty flaky technology and you need to be a bit of a techy. Great for hobbyists etc but if you want to do some serious business you need something better. I am sure there are other options out there. **However Google have moved to "GSuite" and their offering appears far more attractive.**

I have personally used all three of these platforms and by far the most stable and professional is "GoToWebinar" but you pay for it.

You can also record that webinar and then deliver a replay to your visitors.. Now you could also leave your replay on YouTube because it does that and there are lots of other advantages that you might want to take advantage of, especially if you want to make your summit something that you want to circulate to other people on the internet. You can also do your summit on "instant teleseminar". Now, "instant teleseminar" does not show video, so what you'd be doing is you'd be doing an audio summit and this does carry with it some advantages, especially if you want to have people attend by phone, maybe don't have a smart phone, but maybe they like to follow along while they drive or while they're listening in at the gym or someplace where they are stationary.

. There are sites like Periscope, there are also sites like Snapchat and Blab and what this does is this ties directly to sites like Twitter where you are going to be interacting with people on social media and of course you do get the effect of virality or being viral and all we mean by being viral is that you are going to be able to catch other people in the networks of others.

As you began to have your messages shared by the people who are visiting your summit. So you want to take into consideration, you want to deliver the summit, and if you're going to want to have a more private venue, than you want to consider using, "go to webinar", because you're going to be able to then take the recordings and then take them offline and then put them into some kind of private sense where your visitors are going to be able to see it. But if you want it to be public and you want visitors to be able to have access to it indefinitely, you can consider using live streaming apps. Now, the downside to live streaming apps is that you're going to have to work hard and making sure that people will know when each session starts and ends. But for the most part, this is another way of being able to deliver your summit and for you to be able to connect with others while you do it.

OUTSOURCING DURING YOUR SUMMIT

In this chapter we're going to be talking about outsourcing during your summit and this is one thing that typically goes undiscussed when we talk about doing a summit, but it's a very important aspect of making sure that both your presenters and your guests are taken care of and that they have a great experience during your summit. Now every summit has a number of moving parts, but you should be focused on list building and sales. That is the reason why you're doing the summit. So you want to do everything that you can to make sure that again, those visitors are having a great experience and when you have this many details to manage, you want to have someone else take care of the logistics. And what do we mean by logistics? Well, one of the logistics is guest management and this is making sure that the people that are going to be presenting, that if they have slides, that they're ready and in place and if they have a bio link that there that it's going to be shown.

And that the physical webinar with the actual venue is being managed by someone so that you can talk to the guests and you can transition the presenter and so that you know that your guests can, if they have questions that they're going to be answered, so do what you can to have this part outsourced. Now you can get an outsourcer from a virtual assistant pool. You can actually get an assistant that you already have, but of course you can also have someone who wants to be involved with your brand or your business and then just wants to volunteer their time. Again, you just want to make sure that the logistics of managing your guests is really taken care of and that you can actually have someone else do that. Wow. You make sure that the process is going smoothly with the presenters and the attendees.

Great customer service can be outsourced. Now, if you don't already have someone who's managing your customer service and your support, you want to give the visitors a support link and you want to make sure that anything that's going to happen during the summit while it's going on that you were answering those questions quickly and resolving them. Again. If people, for whatever reason for a particular session they can't get in or something is happening or they're getting an error you want, you want to have someone who is managing that process and at least addressing their concerns in real time so that any of the support systems that you're going to manage, whether you have Zen desk, whether you have OS ticket, you want to have someone who is monitoring that support site almost every minute that your summit is in session. This is vital again to the experience of the user. It's vital to the experience of the presenter.

Crowd controls and questions can be outsourced. Anytime someone is having a concern during the actual presentation, you want to manage that concern and sometimes it's rare but you might have a case where you have someone and they're causing a disturbance and they're not necessarily with the programme. You're going to want to have the ability to either eject that person or have someone addressing them while the presentation is happening. You want to keep your focus on the presentation. You want to keep your focus on the guests. So when this is happening, if you have someone who's assisting you, they can address any crowd control issue. They can address anything from someone who is maybe not quite happy with what's happening. So you want to take care of this process if you can and have someone else manage it.

Now lastly, your guests are going to want to have replays and you are going to run into situations where if you make replays available that people are gonna want to see them as soon as possible. Maybe they weren't able to make it at the time that your presentation was held. If you can, the faster you can make those replays available, the better off you're going to be. Now, you don't want to disincentivize people to come to the actual live presentation, but at the same time though, if your goal is to get the content to people than what you have to do is you've got to make sure that those replays get to people and they get to people as soon as that summit is over, having someone who can package the replays, having someone who can edit them if they need to be, having someone who can take the handouts or the slides and get them ready and get all of that taken care of and then put in a place where it can be downloaded and then getting an email out to people.

That's a process and you want to have that process managed. Again, your number one goal here is to make sure that your list is growing. Your number one concern here is that the content is being delivered. Your number one concern is going to be making sure that the people who are attending the summit, they have great things to say that they are sharing it on social media. They are talking about how awesome it is, and if you keep your focus on that and you can do it, if your focus is on these other things that could be outsourced during the summit, then you are not going to be focused on the main thing, the primary goal for which you're having this summit. So consider outsourcing every detail. That has nothing to do with list building. That has nothing to do with making sure that people are having a great experience.

MONETIZATION

In this chapter, we're going to be talking about monetization of your summit. There is going to be several ways for you to be able to monetize the event. There's no right way, there's no wrong way. There's only going to be the way that fits into your business model best. Now of course right off the bat, you can charge up front for the meeting or the entire slate of speakers and this is one way of simplifying everything. Someone pays, they get access to a membership site and then they can sign up for the webinars. The links are all there and again, everything is really streamlined because people are actually going to become your customer when they buy into the actual summit. Now that does not necessarily build your list any faster, but what it does is it puts buyers into your list, so that's a great way of being able to monetize the event.

Do it upfront and you can also charge once the summit is over for recordings in a multistep offer. Now here is the benefit to that. You will have captured the lead upfront every time someone wants to attend the summit, they will have to put their name and email address into something in order to get access to the link to the webinar. So this is going to be a great way for you to be able to collect leads. And of course you will need to be able to work with them and monetize them through email marketing. But you will have a larger list, but you may or may not have buyers if you are not chqrging upfront.

Now when we talk about giving affiliates and presenters a hundred percent on the whole funnel. what we're talking about is that they're going to actually be incentivize in order to mail their list and to get people to the summit knowing that the product that's going to be sold on the back end is going to be one where they're going to profit and they're gonna be profit all the way. And so when an affiliate can profit from all the steps in the funnel, they may be incentivized to mail. That's going to strengthen your lead list. It's going to give you buyers, even though you will not be monetizing them on the front end. So now you might ask them, how am I going to actually make money from the summit? Well, one of the things you're going to do is once the summit is over, you are going to bring your new attendees onto your list.

Having brought them onto th4 webinar, you are going to then market something to them that's directly related to what they just saw. So this is something, and it probably should be your product. It should be something that came from you. It shouldn't be an affiliate product from either the speakers and it probably really shouldn't be an affiliate product from someone else. You should be marketing something that really is coming from you and your sense of authority. Now the benefit in all of these things is that you will have succeeded in building your list. Now obviously, again, your, your lead list will be smaller if you monetize up front and you charge, but again, it's going to be more focused because you'll already have buyers. But regardless, however you monetize any of the ways that we've just mentioned, you will have succeeded in building your list. Or even if you advertise and you get new people in by Facebook ads or YouTube ads or however you do it, you will have built your list and you will have monetized and you will be able to monetize over and over again because you'll be doing that through email marketing.

REVERSE ENGINEERING THE PROCESS

In conclusion, we're going to talk about what you can do in order to really solidify the things that you've learned about doing a summit. Now we've called this chapter "Reverse Engineering the Process" and the idea here is to find previous online summits that have been done and then to really go behind the details and then to figure out how you want to actually do yours.

Often if you want to do an online summit or anything that is new, you want to try to find other models. You want to try to get a sense for what the guardrails are, what the parameters are, and we're going to talk about how you're going to go about that in this chapter. Now one online summit that you can take a look at is called the best sellers summit and it was done by Ron Douglas and Alice Seba and we'll talk a little bit more about how you're going to go about this, but as you start to do your research, this is a great one and it was actually one where both Ron and Alice charged people upfront and it was considered to be fairly successful and it's one that they are going to be doing on an annual basis.

Another online summit is called the superhero summit. It's done by Marisa Murgatroyd and she's actually done three of these over the last three years depending on when you are watching this video or listening to this audio. Now what you want to do when you look up the superhero summits, each one was different, but this is a summit where attendees were not charged in order to attend the summit live, but when they went to buy the recordings, they did pay a fee of $97 in some cases, and that fee is actually gone up from there. So when you start to look for and do the research on superhero summits, just be aware that this was actually one where affiliates sent traffic but they sent traffic to a page and they sent traffic to the summit where people attend it live. There was the offline summit done by Charles Harper and this was for local marketing consultants.

This was one where people actually paid up front to attend and they were actually given webinars over a period of time. Now let's go into what you're going to do in terms of reverse engineering these case studies and gathering from them the things that you're going to need in order to figure out what it is you want to do in your online summit. So the concept of reverse engineering is also one that's been popularised by marketer, Russell Brunson. He calls it funnel hacking and funnel hacking is really taking a look at everything that another person has done. Taking a look for everything in terms of their advertising, taking a look at everything in terms of how they get their traffic, taking a look at everything in terms of their sales pages, their opt in pages, their upsells, their cross-sales or downsales and anything that's associated with their, with their, with their sales process.

You want to take a look for yourself. Now when we talk about reverse engineering, what are the first things you're going to do actually is to take the name in this summit and you're going to search for the name. Now when you search for the name, you're going to get all the sales pages, you're probably gonna find all the lead up pages and you're actually going to get those pages where people were actually talking the summit up and it's actually going to be a great thing for you to look at because you're going to find out how they publicise some of the summits. So that's going to be a great way for you to find out how you can publicise yours. Now when you actually search for the name of the summit, you were actually going to do a search for two words and you'll do it separately.

One time you're going to do a search for the word JV. Now the reason you're gonna do that is because you want to know how the summit or the product from the summit was promoted when if you can't find anything when you do a search for JV, you'll also want to use the word affiliates. The purpose in doing this is for you to get a sense for the affiliate recruitment page, but also the incentive. What was it that was incentivizing the affiliates to promote the summit? Whether they promote it on the front end or the back end and you want to have a snapshot of all the websites. You want to have them all bookmark and you want to keep them in a file for reference because in terms of trying to design a summit, it's always going to be helpful to use other models and if you hit the wall or you're trying to make a decision, you want to take a look at those summits and the already been successful. We've already listed some, of course they're going to be others, but whenever you are researching them, start by looking to see if there was affiliate traffic that was directed to that summit.

Now you're also going to want to take a look at the payment platform. The most popular two are going to be JVZoo and warrior plus. You want to find the exact product and you want to take a look at the actual funnel. You want to take a look at the upsells. You want to take a look at the down sells if possible. If it's affordable, you want to buy their summit product and this will give you a very good glimpse of what you can do. It will give you a glimpse of what you can do in terms of designing the member's area. In terms of designing your autoresponder sequence, you are going to really get a good sense of you can buy the product but certainly if you can't or you don't want to buy the product, looking at the product as if you were going to be affiliate from the payment process in terms of JVZoo or warrior plus, you will be able to tell a lot in terms of how the summit was structured and how it was actually sold in order to monetize.

Of course, when you take a look at the sales process, you want to read thoroughly the sales pages. You want to find out the angle, you want to find out the pitch. You want to find out how it was actually sold, that they use a video in order to sell the summit. Did they use testimonials? What were the angles of the testimonials? Do your research at this point because this will help you to formulate a successful summit. All the JV pages, all the squeeze pages and opt in pages. Did, they use exit pops.? All of those things are things that you want to note in detail.

One thing that you'll also want to do here is you want to do a little research on the JVs because in some cases, if the JV is in the same niche that you are, or the affiliate may want to tell them that you have a similar summit that you're doing that you'd like their help on. Now of course, you don't want to wait until the day before the summit when you're reaching out to people. Again, as always, you want to be establishing relationships long before you decide to do a summit because these are going to be the people that are not are going to be your presenters, but they're also going to be some of the people that As you start to do your reverse engineering and really looking at each particular part, you're going to want to apply different pieces to what it is that you are going to want to do.

ABOUT THE AUTHOR

Leonard Payne is retired and living on the edge of the Peak District in Derbyshire England. He lives with his wife and he spends his time as an independent publisher. He says that it keeps him in fine wine and cheese in his old age.

www.ingramcontent.com/pod-product-compliance
Lightning Source LLC
Chambersburg PA
CBHW030548220526
45463CB00007B/3030